NIHIL OBSTAT:

Rev Canon William Young MA PhB STL
Catholic Diocese of Brentwood
England

IMPRIMATUR:

Rev Mgr Canon Kevin W A Hale
Vicar General
Catholic Diocese of Brentwood
England

The Nihil Obstat and Imprimatur are a declaration that this book is free from doctrinal or moral error. It does not imply that those who granted the approval agree with the opinions, contents or statements expressed.

Granted 1st May 2018

First published for distribution June 2018

PG Parental guidance recommended

DEDICATION

This book is dedicated to Our Lady of Walsingham, patroness of England; may she pray that this little book may serve as a means to draw many people to fall "head over heels" in love with her Divine Son Jesus Christ, our greatest Lover!

Ave Maria!

PG Parental guidance recommended

First printed 2018

Re-Printed 2024

Panda Press UK

1, Newcastle Street,

Stone,

ST15 8GU

England

Distributed and sold by Holy Cross Catholic Bookshop, London, England
www.holycrossbooks.co.uk

ISBN: 978-1-7398407-6-1

PG Parental guidance recommended

CONTENTS

PG – Parental guidance recommended

PG Parental guidance recommended

Introduction

Even young people brought up in families whose religious beliefs strongly oppose sex before marriage often find it very difficult to put together any coherent reasons to support their belief. Most of the population is very much in favour of sex before marriage, and opposing this mind-set can feel as absurd as saying the world is flat!

What's more, the reasons proposed to young people in favour of sex before marriage can sound very sensible. Things like "Sleeping around may not be a good idea, but surely committed boyfriend–girlfriend relationships are ok?" or "If you really are in love, then surely making love is a good way to strengthen your relationship?" are very seductive arguments at first glance.

Traditionally, the primary reason for young (fertile) people to avoid sex before marriage has focused on the rights of children. These historical arguments involving the rights of the child started from the premise that anyone who has sex is a possible future parent.

Most people would agree that a good and just society should always put the needs of children first. We all expect formal, legal arrangements when we take out a mortgage on a house, to safeguard the money of the lender. Children, the argument goes, are far more valuable than a house; therefore, the least a child can expect in a good and just society, where the rights of the child are truly put first, is to be born into a secure household, which society has an obligation to protect with formal laws; and this means marriage.

That's not to say that single mothers, unmarried couples,

PG Parental guidance recommended

orphanages, step-parents, fostering services, nuns, etc. cannot do a great job, but the overwhelming evidence shows that the best way for a child to be reared is by a loving mum and dad who have made a publicly stated, lifelong commitment to each other and to any children that they may have. Since having sex implies the realistic possibility of conceiving a child, simple justice requires a child protection strategy, and by far the best child protection strategy is marriage.

The most appalling violation of the rights of the child is termination of pregnancy – abortion. This is a commonly applied "solution" for an "accidental" pregnancy in couples who are not married – and indeed some who are.

Many advocates of abortion have the intellectual honesty to admit that if the statement "I would like to have sex with you" is separated from the statement "I would like to have a baby with you", then abortion must be available as a safety net in case of contraceptive failure. For instance, Ann Furedi, British Pregnancy Advisory Service Chief Executive, the leading UK charity providing abortion, who describes herself on Facebook as pro-choice, humanist and libertarian, has said that abortion, in her view, is necessary because "ultimately women cannot control their fertility through contraception alone, and (*consequently*) they need accessible abortion services as a back-up for when their contraception lets them down."(1)

Sex outside marriage gained widespread acceptance by young people from about 1960 onwards. It did not take long for people, not just Catholics but many others, including left-wing intellectuals, to recognise the serious adverse consequences it was having on children who were born to unmarried women.

To give one example, Professor A. H. Halsey, former Professor of Social Policy at Oxford University and co-author of *English Ethical Socialism*, said: “No one can deny that divorce, separation, birth outside marriage and one-parent families as well as cohabitation and extra-marital sexual intercourse have increased rapidly. Many applaud these freedoms. But what should be universally acknowledged is that the children of parents who do not follow the traditional norm (i.e. taking on personal, active and long-term responsibility for the social upbringing of the children they generate) are thereby disadvantaged in many major aspects of their chances of living a successful life. On the evidence available, such children tend to die earlier, to have more illness, to do less well at school, to exist at a lower level of nutrition, comfort and conviviality, to suffer more unemployment, to be more prone to deviance and crime, and finally to repeat the cycle of unstable parenting from which they themselves have suffered... The evidence all points in the same direction, is formidable, and tallies with common sense.”(2) Marriage is simply what is best for children.

Given the widespread acceptance of sex before marriage as a social norm, in which numerous sexually active, unmarried couples seem very happy, it is understandable that many people can’t see why there is any problem. Furthermore, contraception is frequently seen as 100% safe and as a responsible method of keeping sex and babies separate. Consequently, the thought “These arguments don’t relate to me” can easily enter anyone’s mind-set.

This little book was written in the hope that it will help to explain, beyond the traditional arguments, why sex before marriage is not a good choice.

The book contains explanations from common sense, observational evidence, philosophy, and, where appropriate, empirical scientific research findings. Many individuals and groups may find it a useful resource, including:

- Young adults
- Dating couples
- Parents and guardians
- Those preparing for marriage
- R.E. teachers
- Catechists
- Marriage preparation instructors
- Priests and religious guiding young people

There is a need to overcome fatalism, that is, beliefs such as "Young people will all have sex before marriage anyway, so what's the point?" or "Nobody stops having sex once they start." It's an insult to young people to even suggest that "they will do it anyway". These assumptions are simply wrong; many young people do make a choice and say "No". Human beings should not be lowered to the level of animals, driven by instinct and unable to control their own behaviour.

Parents are the key to education, but many feel completely unprepared for the task. The world around us can offer some seemingly very convincing reasons to go along with the prevailing attitudes. Thus, preparation is essential. St. Peter, the first Pope, wrote: "Always have

PG Parental guidance recommended

your answer *ready* for people who ask you the *reason* for the hope that you all have. But give it with courtesy and respect."(3) Hopefully, this little book is a step on the road of preparation that St. Peter had in mind.

PG Parental guidance recommended

In view of the intimate nature of the subject matter, it is recommended that individuals under the age of 18 seek parental approval before reading the text. Parents are in the best position to know the kindest way to educate their children in all things, and that certainly includes sex.

PG Parental guidance recommended

Chapter 1

What has Jesus got to do with sex anyway?

When Jesus lived on earth, he clearly taught that sex before or outside marriage is a serious impediment to happiness on earth, and a significant obstacle to going to heaven when we die. Jesus specifically condemned fornication, the formal name for sexual intercourse outside of marriage, and licentiousness (indecency), the formal name for acts like masturbation, petting and teasing to cause sexual arousal. This is clearly written in St. Mark's Gospel.(4) He called these things sinful.

The word "sin" these days is not popular, for many reasons. Possibly this is in part because the word has been used too liberally by religious people in the past to subjectively and cruelly label people as bad ("sinners"), when in fact they were suffering from things that involved no personal culpability – for example, psychological guilt disorders, actions performed because of confusion about what was right and wrong, or simply being innocently deceived by others in authority who should have known better.

The word sin means disobeying the will of God. Just as a child disobeys the will of his or her parents by stealing biscuits from the biscuit barrel, a person disobeys God's will, i.e. commits sin, by using sex in ways that he forbids.

PG | Parental guidance recommended

Using the word "sin" in the context of sexual activity is not popular in common parlance, because there is a general loss of awareness of why anything occurring between consenting adults can be an insult to God or offend him.

There are many reasons for this loss of awareness of "sex life" sin. One of the most important is a loss of belief in God as our Father, someone who is very close and wants to be involved in the day-to-day lives of every human being. This is sad, because Jesus revealed by his life that God's love for each of us is like a daddy's love for his son or daughter. The Lord's Prayer starts with "Our Father who art in heaven", but a better rendering to bring out the meaning of the prayer is "Our Daddy who art in heaven"!

As a doctor, I have spoken to many people when they were dying, and I have also accompanied many relatives of people who are dying. It is well known that suffering and death often act as memory agents to re-ignite the understanding that human beings are dependent on God. However, a very common occurrence in our age, even among this extreme cohort of people who have been given the most powerful reminder that life on earth comes to an end, is that God is a distant creator who is "up there", who blindly leaves us to make up our own minds about what is the best way to behave. All too often, God is not seen as a loving daddy who guides his children in all things (as Christianity teaches). If God is believed to be so far away, two people in a bedroom having sex are understandably perceived to be of no concern to God, and therefore mentioning the words "sin" or "disobedience" seems like a nonsense.

But when God is known as a daddy, then it immediately

PG Parental guidance recommended

becomes much clearer, since even a human daddy is very concerned about what happens to his little princess or superhero, and especially concerned about anything or anyone that can harm them!

What's more, it is the job of a loving daddy to decide for his child what is good and what is bad. The child does not make the rules about "goodness". This is why our self-invented ideas of "I am good" do not make much sense, since we have no reliable way of defining what "goodness" really is.

Another way of seeing it is that we are made by a loving creator. Just like a washing machine works and functions well if the manufacturer's instructions are followed, so too with us and our supernatural manufacturer-God. If a washing machine is used contrary to the instructions printed on the side of the machine, all manner of problems arise. So too with us; if we do not follow the law of the maker printed in our nature, we cannot experience the full working order that God wants us to experience.

All this analysis, of course, depends upon the credibility of Jesus, who claimed that he was God made man. Is Jesus himself the clearest proof that God loves us like a daddy? This is essential if we are to accept him as a guide in questions of good sexual behaviour. Is Jesus worth listening to?

Firstly, some might say that in any case, Jesus was living on earth more than 2,000 years ago, when things were very different, so perhaps his advice concerning sex before marriage should change to catch up with the modern world?

PG Parental guidance recommended

Indeed, many things were different 2,000 years ago. Yet, when it comes to issues concerning sexual behaviour, things were not that different. Certainly, sex before marriage was a hot topic. Among the biggest pieces of evidence to support this are the historical records documenting the accusations made against Mary, the mother of Jesus. Mary claimed that the birth of Jesus came about by the miraculous intervention of God: the virgin birth. Many of her detractors alleged she was just a sexually active single young woman. For example, the pagan historian Celsus recorded that some people who lived at the same time as Mary claimed that she simply had sex before marriage with a Roman soldier called Panthera, as this was not a particularly rare event in the lives of people under Roman dominion.(5)

Jesus Christ claimed to be God.(6) The New Testament is full of direct and indirect claims made by Jesus that he was divine (this means God). Perhaps the most famous is the beginning of the Gospel of St. John: "In the beginning was the Word: the Word was with God and the Word was God." St. John goes on to say that Jesus is "the Word made flesh" (human). If Jesus is God, then that makes him the best advisor we can get. God is the all-knowing being. But was Jesus correct when he claimed to be God made man? There are many people in our psychiatric hospitals right now who make similar claims, and we do not believe them, and we certainly would not go to them for advice concerning our sex lives. The question is, then, is Jesus truly God made man?

Jesus taught us that God always wants to be united with human beings for eternity in a perfectly happy, loving union. That happy and loving union is called heaven. It is a free, undeserved gift from God to us. God does not need to share his happiness, but he has chosen to do so. In fact, God loves us so much that he leaves us free, meaning we can freely decide to seek our happiness elsewhere. That may, at first glance, appear an odd choice. After all, why would anybody refuse a gift of infinite happiness forever? Surely, everybody would choose immense happiness, i.e. heaven. On the other hand, it sounds like a very nasty God who makes people but does not automatically share his happiness with them.

Yet, this way of seeing things may not be correct. Any truly loving relationship must involve free choice. This is clear even in our human friendships. We may be very kind to a friend, but he or she can respond either positively or negatively to our kindness. In religious language, a positive response to God's invitation to friendship is called having faith.

Faith in another is believing that that person has the best message for our happiness. Religious faith acknowledges not just that God exists but also that we depend on him. Even the Devil believes God exists, but this is not faith.

Sadly, an all-too-common example of a person not having faith in a good-willed person, and choosing to seek happiness elsewhere, are the millions of cases of a dedicated wife who does everything for her husband, only to find him in the arms of a mistress. The adulterer has placed his faith in finding happiness in another woman. In the English language, we commonly call this being unfaithful.

Hence, it is possible to imagine (mistakenly) that greater happiness can be found away from God, and to choose to go elsewhere. Having faith in God means believing that

He alone offers our best opportunity for happiness. Having faith is an essential requirement for forming a relationship with God, just as having faith and being faithful is an essential requirement for forming a marriage. God is not being nasty by making people and not automatically giving them heaven; he is being loving by permitting people to walk away. Love has to allow free choice; otherwise, it would be a dictatorship.

If Jesus is God, then what he said is true. And just as the maker of a car knows best how to make the car run optimally, so too the Maker of human beings knows what the best way to live is.

But was Jesus right when he claimed to be God? Maybe Jesus was a liar, simply mistaken or just mad? It is essential to know for sure whether Jesus is God or not, otherwise his counsel about sex (and more importantly, about all the things we need to do to get to heaven) is of no more use than the counsels of any other advisor.

Jesus had the title Son of God. In the Jewish vocabulary, this was a clear claim to be God. In English, being a son of England can just mean I was born in England, or it can mean I have all the attributes of an English person. Jesus meant the latter when he accepted the title Son of God. He meant that he was God. He was executed for saying it!

To prove that he was God, Jesus said he would give up his life voluntarily and then by his own supernatural power rise from the dead.(7) Supernatural in this sense means events that reverse the laws of nature. In nature, when a body is dead, it is dead forever. While miracles such as healing the sick can happen, and the miracles that Jesus worked were real, these events can also be deceptions.

PG Parental guidance recommended

However, the one that is the miracle of miracles, showing that supernatural power is at work, is coming back from the dead. The dead cannot deceive; dead human bodies cannot by any scientific explanation come back to life.

The early believers in Christianity looked very carefully at the evidence for the crucifixion and resurrection before giving it their adherence. They knew this belief is the keystone that supports all the other truths of Christianity. They checked out the questions “Did he really die?” and “Did he really rise from the dead?” with meticulous scrutiny.

The resurrection question was one that was debated from the time of the crucifixion of Christ, around 33 A.D., onwards. For example, the Talmud, which is a Jewish religious and historical document written around 200 A.D., clearly talks about the “false claim” (false in the eyes of the Jewish religious authorities) of the bodily resurrection of Jesus. It was therefore a belief that was not just written down by Christians.(8) The Christian writings in the New Testament of the Bible are also supported as historical documents by archaeological findings at biblical sites.(9)

Sceptics, of course, tend to discount the biblical accounts because they consider the Bible is “just a religious book”. But that is not true. In addition to the Word of God, the Bible is also, in many parts, a book of history, documenting the actual events of that time in history by eyewitness accounts. It has numerous references to historical events that have been corroborated by modern historical research. For example, many people used to think that the Bible had many historical errors in it, such as Luke’s statement that Lysanias was the tetrarch of

Abilene in about A.D. 27.(10) For hundreds of years, scholars used this "factual error" to prove Luke was wrong because it was common knowledge that Lysanias was the ruler of Chalcis, a long way off. But an archaeological inscription uncovered in the 20th century said that Lysanias was the tetrarch of Abilene at the time that Luke reported. It turns out that there had been two people name Lysanias, and Luke had indeed recorded the facts accurately.(11)

The Bible always speaks the truth in different ways – just as we experience in our modern world. For instance, both poetry and scientific journals can talk about love in ways that are very different, even though each is as truthful as the other.(12) In some places, the Bible is obviously also using language that is symbolic and not literal. Bible history can be real time or symbolic time.

Real-time Bible history says, from eyewitness accounts, that Jesus Christ died and then three days later rose from the dead. His death is rarely disputed; Roman soldiers knew how to crucify – there were no survivors. Indeed, numerous non-Christian writers testify to the death of Jesus on the cross.(13) Crucifixion was an imported method of execution that had been invented in Persia (modern-day Iran) 400 years before Christ. The Romans used the technique because they could not find one that matched it for cruelty, humiliation (the victim was naked) and effectiveness at ensuring a protracted, painful death.

But sceptics will still refuse to accept the resurrection of Jesus, coming up with hypothetical theories to explain it away. The most common of these theories is the claim that the disciples merely stole the body of Jesus and hid it, and then lied to people by telling them that he really rose from the dead. Other attempts at explaining the resurrection as a made-up story make the acronym TRASHED:

Twin- the idea that a person who looked like Jesus and claimed to be Jesus got crucified.
Robbery- the idea that the body was stolen.
Allegorical- the idea Jesus meant his resurrection was a symbolism simply of a new way of living.
Swooning- the idea that Jesus pretended to be dead.
Hallucination- the idea the witnesses were all just seeing something that did not really exist due to an illness.
Ethanol- the idea the witnesses were all high on alcohol or psychogenic drugs to explain a mass hallucination.
Deception- the idea it was just all a big lie.

Let us examine the evidence for or against the resurrection of Jesus by looking at a series of questions:

If Jesus did not actually rise from the dead, why did the disciples change from being frightened, timid followers of Jesus before his death, into bold evangelists willing to die for preaching his resurrection?

Remember, before Jesus was crucified, the disciples were, for the most part, cowards. Before the crucifixion, Peter denied even knowing Jesus three times. What event changed them from cowards into brave men? Answer: They must have actually seen the risen Jesus.

Why were the disciples willing to be tortured and killed for what they knew was a lie – if they had really just made the whole thing up and he was still dead?

PG Parental guidance recommended

You do not need a degree in human psychology to know that people do not die for a cause they know to be false. People do certainly die for false beliefs all the time, but only when they think they are dying for the truth. If the disciples faked the resurrection, or Jesus meant it as a symbolism of a change of behaviour they would know Christianity is a lie because Jesus said literally he would die and rise again. History records they were tortured and killed for their faith, and not one of them said, under torture, "Okay, okay, we made the whole thing up." Why is that? Answer: They must have really seen the risen Jesus.

What was the motive of the early believers in Jesus Christ?

Lies or deceptions are typically done for some selfish motive. Preaching the resurrection of Jesus would not bring them wealth, fame, status, or popularity. It would only cause them to be hated, scorned, persecuted, excommunicated from their previous religion, imprisoned, exiled, beheaded, tortured, and crucified, as history records. What could possibly be their motive? Just to save face? That is certainly not logical. No one is going to go through what the disciples went through just because they are too embarrassed to say, "I guess we were wrong." So, what was their motive? Answer: It was the truth. They must have seen the risen Jesus.

How did the Apostles, 12 ordinary people, pull off such a "hoax"?

Remember, this "hoax" would trigger thousands of sceptics per day to convert to following their "fraud" as well as redirecting the entire world to even eventually

PG Parental guidance recommended

change the calendar, and establish their hoax character, Jesus, as the best-known religious figure in all humanity. How could they pull something like this off without ever getting exposed, offering a deathbed confession or even admitting it was a hoax under torture? Answer: They must have actually seen the risen Jesus.

Why would thousands of people immediately convert if Jesus didn't really rise from the dead?

History records that thousands upon thousands were converted instantly and immediately to be followers of Jesus, as many as 3,000 in a single day. It is reported in Acts 1:3 and 1 Corinthians 15:6 that after the crucifixion, Jesus appeared alive over a span of 40 days and to "500 brethren". Back then, only men were counted in crowd totals, so factoring in women and children, Jesus most likely appeared to around 1,500 to 2,000 people over 40 days. If that many people saw Jesus alive, it would explain how so many were converted, because even the most hardened sceptics would have crowds and crowds of former sceptics saying, "Yes, it's true! We've all seen him too!" But if no one saw him alive and the crowds had only the words of the disciples to go by, why would thousands convert?

Remember, the disciples were preaching to many who did not want to believe Jesus was the Messiah. What words could they speak to hostile crowds to convince them Jesus really did rise from the dead? "Trust us?" That might convince some of the disciples' closest friends, but not thousands upon thousands of sceptics. So why did thousands convert? Answer: Crowds of people must have actually seen the risen Jesus, it was not a symbolic event.

PG Parental guidance recommended

Why did the disciples make themselves look bad in the Gospels?
Think about it: If you were going to make up a story, wouldn't you present yourself in a somewhat positive light? The disciples painted themselves in the Gospels as cowards lacking in faith. They told how they had run away and denied Christ. Why? Answer: They must have been telling the truth.

How could the disciples even steal the body in the first place?

The body was encased in a tomb with a 24-hour watch by guards authorised by the Roman governor and trained to kill. The punishment for breaking a Roman grave seal, or attempting to steal a body, or overpowering a Roman soldier, was death. Thus, how did timid, cowardly disciples muster up the courage to try this?

Furthermore, the stone covering a wealthy Jewish tomb (the site of his burial) weighed about 2 tons. The notion that people came and rolled away the stone while the guards were perhaps asleep is ridiculous. Yet, this was the common story used to explain away the event by non-believers of the time. It is worthwhile remembering that in the armed forces of the time, a serious dereliction of duty had the death penalty attached, so no group of guards would permit this. So how did the stone move, and the body leave the tomb? Answer: A supernatural, miraculous event occurred, something which is beyond any natural, day-to-day, scientifically explained events.

If the body of Jesus was stolen from the grave rather than resurrected, why were the Apostles not executed for the crime?

PG | Parental guidance recommended

The Apostles openly preached about the resurrection in full view of the Roman and Jewish authorities within weeks of the Crucifixion. If the occupying Roman authorities had any evidence that their jurisdiction had been undermined by an assault on their soldiers at the grave or that their law regarding grave robbery had been broken, they would have had no hesitation in punishing the culprits. The Romans were not known for their gentleness! For example, in 70 A.D., they killed an estimated 1.5 million Jewish men, women and children following a revolt against Roman rule. No amount of "hush" money could prevent the authorities from punishing a group of people publicly saying that Jesus was alive if the official story was that they robbed the grave and made up a story. If this were overlooked, then the credibility of the occupying power would have been undermined in the minds of the subject people.

If the Gospel accounts of the resurrection were fabricated, why were women witnesses quoted as the primary witnesses of the resurrection?

In the ancient world, women were not respected as witnesses. In formal legal processes, they were not even allowed to give evidence. But the Gospel writers reported that the first witnesses of the resurrection of Jesus were women because it was the truth, and only the truth mattered. They must have seen the risen Jesus.

Was it all mass hallucination?

The power of suggestion on large crowds is quite remarkable. Undoubtedly, if a sufficiently convincing individual shouted, "Look, there's Jesus!" the

PG Parental guidance recommended

phenomenon of mass hallucination could occur. But what works against this idea is that while that can indeed happen, the reports about Jesus after the resurrection came from multiple locations, multiple numbers of people, individuals, and groups and even people like St. Paul who were actively seeking to destroy Christianity. Therefore, reports of the resurrection cannot be explained away by a supposed mass hallucination.

Maybe God put a Jesus lookalike on the cross and the real Jesus kept himself under cover?

The problem with this theory is that Jesus' arrest, trial, and execution were all done in the presence of hundreds of people, so a switch of persons becomes impossible. Also, both the Jewish and the Roman authorities had no motive to punish the wrong man. And the lookalike would have had to be mad not to shout out, "You've got the wrong man!" This explanation of events is just not credible. Apart from anything else, it involves the all-good God in a lie. Jesus of Nazareth was truly killed and buried. The man the witnesses claimed to see risen from the tomb was the same Jesus of Nazareth who had died.

There have been many religious leaders who have taught knowledge of some very important truths. But all these people asked the question, "Do you believe in my teaching?" Christ is different – he asks everybody, "Do **you** believe in me? Do **you** believe that I am your God, your Creator? If he was not who he claimed to be, he should be cast aside as a dangerous man. But if he is who he claimed to be, reason dictates that everything he taught as the supreme intelligence is true and worthy of adherence, since sensible people respond to wisdom. This is why Catholics listen to Jesus when he talks about sex.

PG | Parental guidance recommended

Chapter 2

Surely what matters to God is being a good person, not what goes on in the bedroom?

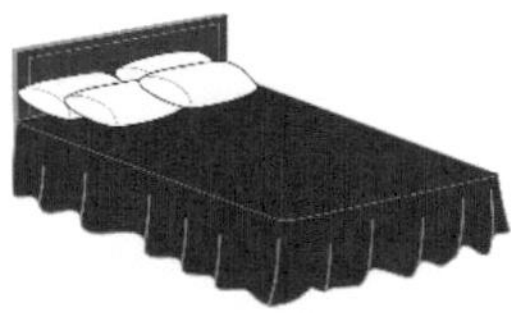

Why does Jesus care what goes on in the bedroom? Because Jesus is God and he clearly revealed the nature of God by his life on earth. He revealed that God is love, and therefore, as a true lover, he wants what is best for us in everything that we do, and that includes our sexual lives.

The sexual life is an opportunity for great joy but also great pain, as shown by any casual reading of relationship problem pages in magazines, or attendance at a general practitioner doctors' surgery, often frequented by those suffering the painful breakdown of a sexually active relationship.

In the world that Jesus lived in, there was great poverty, cruelty, social injustice, racism, sexism and every other category of "ism" that are correctly highlighted nowadays as issues that demand attention. But Jesus did not say, for example, "Let's first eradicate material poverty, and sexual morality can take a backseat." Jesus called for a radical change of the whole person.

The question of why Jesus cares about what goes on in the bedroom really points to the deeper question: why do we

PG Parental guidance recommended

need Jesus as a helper and a guide in any part of our lives? Why do we need a helper and guide (what is traditionally called a saviour)?

The name Jesus means “Saviour”, a person who saves others. Saving is a word that is not commonly used nowadays to signify bringing about a radical change in another person. It is perhaps more usual to talk about “transforming” someone. Jesus is a transformer in modern speak.

If anybody has ever said to you that you are perfect just the way you are, you know that in fact they are lying to you! Just think of the times when perhaps you’ve spoken harshly about others behind their backs, the times when you cheated on a friend, the times when you told lies, the times when you failed to help a person close to you in need of your help, or, in the context of this book, the times when you perhaps acted in a sexual way that used another person manipulatively.

All of these actions, and many more, show that we each need to be changed into a new person, to be transformed. And trying to transform ourselves without anyone’s help just does not work.

It is popularly thought that the “goodness” of a person is about public activity; what goes on in private between consenting individuals is not an issue. It is commonly believed that if you live a life full of public good works, then you are a good person and when you die you deserve to go to heaven. However, there are a few things wrong with the idea that goodness is about the public life of the individual, and that going to heaven and being happy forever when we die is purely a matter of our own effort.

PG Parental guidance recommended

In the private life of the bedroom, many lesser or greater failings manifest as reasons to question a person's "goodness". Cheating, lies about one's true feelings, using others for mere gratification, emotional manipulation leading a partner into sexual acts that they do not want to perform, or placing pressure on one's partner to have sex when what they really want is to be cherished as a person not a sex provider, are just a few examples of how the real man or woman acts against "goodness" even in private. And if this is how we can treat those with whom we have close, intimate relations, it is absurd to think such an approach won't infect our relationships with other people we meet, be they family, social or professional.

Some people are sexually liberal and are also involved in many visible activities that potentially serve the wellbeing of people around them. That could lead us to conclude that the bedroom is a private matter that does not have any bearing on one's "goodness". But on close analysis, this is not true. The issue comes down to what is best for them and best for those around them. The millionaire who donates to charity and also spreads sexually transmitted diseases is not a great asset to the victims who catch herpes. Similarly, a lonely single mother is not helped by the knowledge that the absent unfaithful father of her child is a great donor to charity in the third world or simply known as a "nice bloke" in the local community. A great political leader who sleeps around and neglects any children he fathers is destroying society despite developing national prestige. The family of a loving mum and dad committed to staying together for life and to supporting their children is the bedrock of a happy society. No political revolution can bring about the sense of wellbeing a child gets from knowing that his or her mum and dad put him or her as number one and will always do so.

Robert Louis Stevenson's famous book *The Strange Case of Dr. Jekyll and Mr. Hyde* reveals something within all of us that helps explain why we need a saviour.(14) It is a book about a split personality in one body, the good Jekyll and the bad Hyde. If we are honest about ourselves, the "me" that appears to others is not the full, real "me" who has weaknesses and flaws which remain hidden from common view. In other words, there is a bit of Mr Hyde in all of us, which we try to keep hidden because we do not like this bit of our character, as it causes shame.

About 2,000 years ago, a fellow-struggler called St. Paul who was one of the first Bishops of the Catholic Church summed it up like this: "Instead of doing the good things I want to do, I carry out the sinful things I do not want. When I act against my will, then, it is not my true self doing it, but sin which lives in me."(15) Both by intrinsic damage to our human nature and by our own choices, things are just not quite right. And we need some help to make things better; our own efforts alone are just not enough.

All human beings yearn deep in their hearts to be the person they know they should be and find deep inner peace. This is clear because most have the honesty to say, "I'm not perfect," implying that the status quo does not satisfy their deep desire for something better. And to repeat a common scenario – if someone tells us that we are perfect just the way we are, they are telling us a lie. And deep down we know it. Every time we feel a twinge of guilt, shame, or plain misgiving over something we've said or done, we are revealing that we secretly feel we are not what we should be.

So, what to do? We sometimes have a tendency to mute the desire to be a better person, the person we want to be, by using distractions to silence the voice inside calling us to change. Things like excessive entertainment, TV, shopping, the iPhone, social media, possessions, gadgets, computer games, and a host of other readily available distractions come to mind. And in the list, sex has to be included, as it has a powerful ability to divert a person from other duties of life. Other common things also contribute to the tendency to run away from the call to change. For example, things like a facade of casual humour, giving the impression all is well, sublimation in charity work to convince oneself "I am good" or even frank denial that there is any problem with "me" – the problems of the world are due to "society". But ultimately, it is practically impossible to silence the small voice inside saying, "I need to be a better and happier person."

Fortunately, Christianity teaches that God wants to help us because God *is* love(16) and God *is* mercy.(17) God does not decide to be these things, he *is* these things. It is just like we are mammals; it is not a choice on our part. Jesus came to earth to make these things about the nature of God crystal clear.

Jesus loves us so much that in every part of our lives he wants to save us from disaster, and that includes saving us in our sexual relations. We are too valuable in the eyes of God to be left on our own. In all areas of our lives, including in the bedroom, we find it very difficult on our own to avoid doing harm either to ourselves or to others. Jesus is there to save us!

PG | Parental guidance recommended

Jesus saves us just as a doctor saves his or her patients. He does this by lovingly instructing us on the ways to live a happy life, and when things do go wrong, he mercifully offers the medicine to make us well again. In religious language we call the love and mercy that saves us from disaster, “grace”. God loves us so much that he offers healing from the time we are born until we die, in all aspects of our lives – including the bedroom!

In the era in which we live many seek help from psychological tools like mindfulness, cognitive behavioural therapy or psychoanalysis. These are all fine if they bring the person to thank God for using these therapies to effect change for the better. However, they are disasters if they are used to convince a person in the power of self alone to effect a change for the better. This is called “selfism” Reliance on the power of self is absurd because it denies the reality that we are all weak and damaged in one way or another and weak damaged beings should not be relied upon to construct strong and untarnished beings. We need a source of perfection and that is God!

Chapter 3

Isn't this "no-sex-before-marriage" stuff just old-fashioned nonsense?

Calling "no sex before marriage" old-fashioned nonsense is very understandable, given the fact that sex before (and outside) marriage is so prevalent in our society.

Around 1960, a big change in sexual behaviour took place in the developed world. It has been called the "sexual revolution". For young people in the UK today, the world after the "sexual revolution" is the only world they know. Within the space of a few years, from about 1960 onwards, there were big changes in the beliefs of most of the population regarding sex.

All changes in behaviour are the result of principles. If a person believes the principle that violence is good, then that person is likely to start fights. If a person believes stealing is good, they are likely to rob Barclays Bank. The principle of the sexual revolution was that any restriction on sexual activity for consenting adult persons is unhealthy for the individual person themselves, their relationships, and society. Before the sexual revolution, the guiding principle was that sexual behaviour needs to be confined to a lifelong, committed relationship between a man and a woman, which we call marriage. The big question is, which principle leads to the most happiness?

The reasons for the huge change in behaviour in a large part of the population are undoubtedly numerous, and nobody can say with absolute certainty the cause or causes. Significant contributory factors were probably attitudes towards women that were never Catholic teaching but did creep into Catholic practice and compromised the proper meaning of a number of rights. These included attitudes towards things like:

- Conjugal Rights: The meaning of the right of a husband to have sex with his wife was not communicated frequently or forcefully enough as the "right to invite" sexual intercourse with one's wife. The impression of too many men was that a conjugal right was an automatic "right to sexual delight" whenever he decided. The language of marital debt was used, and this was interpreted as a debt that is paid on demand, not a debt to be "paid" by mutual reciprocal consensual love.

- Employment Rights: Limitations were commonly placed on women's legitimate aspirations to work outside the home if they so wished. "A woman's place is always in the home, and this is the law of God" was a frequently espoused philosophy.

- Reproductive Rights: Too many women were used as baby factories. A large family is a great blessing, but it demands the cooperation of the couple in deciding what is the best number of children for them to maximise their love. For some couples even having one child may be more than they can handle, for others having ten children is a source of great joy. Unfortunately, in the past, too many women were not part of the decision-making process about how many

PG Parental guidance recommended

children they should aim for in the marriage. There was a machismo culture ingrained into many marriages. This meant that the size of the family, and especially if it included many boys, was perceived as a measure of the husband's manliness.

- Single Parent Rights: The relatively few women who did conceive a child outside of marriage before 1960 were sometimes treated with a complete lack of charity. A lifetime of scorn and ill-treatment often lay ahead of them and their child or children.

- Marital Separation Rights: If a woman was being abused in her marriage, there was a tendency for some to say she ought to submit to this and live in the same house as her abusing husband regardless of the personal cost, even if it included violence. Marital separation was portrayed as a failure on the part of the woman, rather than being, in many instances, a heroic and justified effort to protect herself and her children.

- Equality Rights: For every single mother who heroically cared for her child, there was a single father who was often not doing all that he should. This obvious fact was often conveniently forgotten, and single mothers alone were labelled as sexually irresponsible, promiscuous, and damaging to family life and the correct ordering of society.

- Home-maker Rights: Too often in the past, the person who went out to work and earned money was seen as the most important contributor to the stability of the family and to society at large. Usually the woman, as the housewife, was undervalued, instead of being seen as an equal partner doing an essential job of raising the next generation and building a home that ensured that the man could function efficiently. Being labelled as a secondary, inconsequential figure could lead to understandable perceptions of worthlessness on the part of the wife. The money she received was seen as a gift from her husband, and not as a just share of the pooled family resources.

With problems like these (and many others), it is not surprising that some people looked for another way to regulate sexual activity. Unfortunately, the results of the sexual revolution, and the method adopted, have been very damaging for society, causing millions of people immense pain. Just consider a few statistics:

- Over 1 in 10 people in the UK have had a sexually transmitted disease, and among 25-34 year olds this rises to 1 in 5.(18)
- The divorce rate for first marriages in the UK is greater than 1 in 3.(19)
- The number of women having an abortion in the UK during their lifetime has reached 1 in 3.(20)
- 1.6 million children are cared for by single mothers in the UK.(21)
- The concurrency rate (two or more sexual partners at one time, usually done by surreptitious cheating), is well over 10% and rising.(22)

There are of course (looking at these numbers with the eyes of a scientist) many reasons for escalating rates including different means of reporting, different tests, different definitions of the statistics used, etc. Besides, the mere fact that x correlates with y does not necessarily mean that the cause of x is certainly y. But thrown into

PG Parental guidance recommended

the mix to explain these awful statistics is a massive change of behaviour following the sexual revolution. These things did not occur to anything like this degree before 1960. If you don't believe it, just go and look up the statistics yourself and you will have the proof. For example, abortion was illegal in 1960 and although, sadly, illegal abortions took place, the number of abortions was nowhere near the 200,000 plus per year that are now performed in the UK. The divorce rate stayed approximately constant at around 6% of first marriages until the 1960s, when the rates escalated to the current levels of over 33%. The number of children living in single-parent households has increased dramatically since the 1960s. Approximately 3% of children under 18 lived with a single parent in 1960. And as for sexually transmitted infections, today's newspapers are full of reports on a regular basis about the escalating epidemic that is infecting the young.

SEX BUG EXPLOSION HITS GIRLS UNDER 25

Tough new strain of STI

Whatever your views are about sex, if you really care about the happiness and wellbeing of yourself, your friends, family and fellow citizens, you don't want to see them suffer sexually transmitted infections, suffer the pain of marital breakdown, or undergo the dilemma or trauma of abortion. You don't want to see cheating as part and parcel of many close relationships, or see many young women heroically trying to bring up children by themselves without the day-to-day support of the

PG | Parental guidance recommended

children's father, support which he owes them in justice. Clearly, something has gone badly wrong!

So was everything perfect in the past? No way! The value of women and their place in society as truly equal partners of men must be continuously addressed. But women's liberation is not achieved by permissive sex. This is so true that some of the most militant feminists of the early days of the sexual revolution who espoused free love (sex when and where you want it) now honestly admit that this so-called freedom has all too frequently facilitated male pleasure at no cost to the man in terms of responsibility towards the woman. For example, in 1970 Germaine Greer, who is still alive today, published her book *The Female Eunuch*.(23) It is required reading in most Women's Studies courses as a promotor of the values of sex divorced from marriage. Greer recommended "deliberate promiscuity" without pregnancy as a means of fulfilment. Just fourteen years later, seeing the effects of her beliefs, she profoundly modified her views. In her book *Sex and Destiny*, while certainly not embracing the radical teaching of Jesus, she nevertheless extolled the virtue of chastity (sexual self-control) and declared permissiveness (sex whenever anyone wants it) to be a mistake for both men and women.(24)

The essential point is that the sexual revolution has not led to more happiness but more suffering. "No sex before marriage" is not old-fashioned nonsense, but an important truth that can be readily seen by anyone who is prepared to look at the evidence with unbiased eyes.

PG Parental guidance recommended

Chapter 4

Only an idiot would buy a car without trying it out first. Isn't sex the same?

First off, the idea of "Try before you buy" can sound very sensible. Similar slogans like "Practice makes perfect" or "To find the best you need to try the rest" can seem like a practical approach to sexual behaviour, that will bring the best results for all concerned.

But people are not objects or commodities to be tried out like cars. People have rights and feelings, and taking a human being for a test ride to see if they're worth keeping is an insult. Objects are used and thrown away when they are no use. People who know what true love is don't do this to other human beings; they are too valuable.

And if two people both agree to use each other for their own gratification, then it's an even sadder state of affairs, because both are prepared to risk harming the other person in the pursuit of their own pleasure.

There is much more to the issue than the question, "If both parties agree to sex without ties, what's the problem?" In any transaction, there are more people involved than the two who make the deal. Private deals

PG Parental guidance recommended

are signs to third parties around them of how people are prepared to behave. Human beings are made that way. We are all influenced by what we see going on around us. Therefore, we all have a responsibility to the people outside the bedroom who are "watching". Our choices matter to others, whether we like it or not. The fact that the actions of some influence the actions of others is clear when one sees the mimicking of celebrity culture that goes on in the lives of thousands of young (and not so young) people.

In many areas of life, practice does make perfect. But sex is not one of them. This is because sex is not meant to be a performance that is scored on a TV talent show. A mother loves her child by loving, learning from day one how to give all of herself for the wellbeing of her child. She may make mistakes along the way, but she is trying, willing to love – she is loving. It would be insulting and harmful if a mother used a child to practise on and make mistakes, and then felt proud that she could now love her own child better. It is the same with boyfriends and girlfriends who really want to love in the proper sense of the word.

It is wise to remember that the primary purposes of dating are to ask oneself two questions. Firstly, is this the person who could be my lifelong soulmate? Secondly, is this the person who I would like to be the parent of my children? The question is she/he good at sex is not important. If the answer to the two key questions is no after a few months of dating, then it is time to move on. When you are in the business of finding a spouse, your happiness and the happiness of your future spouse and your children is not assured by a "try it all before you buy" strategy.

PG Parental guidance recommended

Chapter 5

Surely sex is just sex, no problem?

A common point of view is that if a couple wish to link marriage and sex, that is fine for them, but if others want to keep them separate, then there's no problem.

There is a lot of debate in the scientific literature about sexual desire.(25) Researchers ask, is sexual desire simply an urge like hunger that needs to be satisfied, and then a sense of calm is re-established? Or is sexual desire an emotion, where the wellbeing of the person is safeguarded in the context of a secure relationship? Research really shows what the man in the street already knows – sex can be relegated to a mere physical urge, but this is only done by making an effort, to lesser or greater degrees, to prevent any emotional involvement.

Repressing one's emotions is not good for the psyche. Nobody really thinks it is good to bottle up or deny one's feelings. If people try to convince themselves that they do not care for the person they are having sex with, then it prevents them from understanding themselves, because one's emotions exist to serve a purpose, offering new perspectives and a broader understanding of one's whole self.

Conversely, to let the emotional attachment develop in the context of an insecure relationship is a sure recipe for grief. Human sadness is a very powerful emotion that can have a lifetime's worth of adverse consequences.

For sex to offer the best for the participants, there needs to be a special commitment on the part of each of them. Think of a mother feeding her baby. While many believe that the mother's urge to feed her hungry, crying baby is merely instinctive, it is really much more than an instinct. It is through a close, intimate emotional relationship with a commitment to lifelong attachment, not a quick suckle on the breast, that the most fulfilment is achieved for both mother and child.

Of course, this analysis is over-simplistic. There is a spectrum of commitment ranging from one-night stands to committed boyfriends/girlfriends, engaged couples and married couples. You may be thinking that the above reflections may apply if someone is "sleeping around", but what about couples who are in stable relationships? Surely sex for them has an equivalent value to married sex? What harm does it do?

There seem to be lots of very happy unmarried couples who are having sex. However, "seem" is the operative word here. Firstly, because there is an obvious risk to the person's wellbeing if the relationship ends. It is also reasonable to wonder how "stable" any non-marital sexual relationship is (suspicion regarding the honesty of the other partner is sadly very common). Furthermore, what happens if a child is conceived? And apart from

PG Parental guidance recommended

these three aspects, there is another vital consideration: that of the common good.

In any truly just society, the actions of its citizens should work towards the common good, that is to protect and help the most vulnerable. For this reason, the behaviour of the most powerful should serve to encourage the weaker members of society. What can we expect, for example, of a lonely, vulnerable, poor teenage girl living in a high-rise block of flats when faced with a decision about sex before marriage on a Friday evening, if the more fortunate members of society (e.g. film stars, rock stars, sportsmen, and perhaps you) don't set an example?

The importance of being a role model cannot be overstated. Advantaged individuals have resources of resilience to protect themselves from the damaging effects and allure of many detrimental behaviours, including pre-marital sex. The argument centres on the MAVIS effect, an acronym for:

- Moneyed
- Attractive
- Vivacious (fun-loving)
- Intelligent
- Sexually appealing

Moneyed, Attractive, Vivacious, Intelligent and Sexually appealing individuals on the whole have many psychological, physical and financial resources to protect

PG Parental guidance recommended

themselves in one way or another from the damaging effects of sex with a person who says, “I want to have sex with you and be with you tonight” and not, “I want to have a baby with you and be with you for life.”

That group of people can protect themselves from the adverse effects of many other danger-filled pleasure-seeking activities far better than less fortunate individuals. The power of attractiveness, for example, is very well known and is put into a variety of catchy phrases including “Honey Money”.(26) It is alleged that possibly 50% of lifetime income is dependent upon the power of appearance. If attractiveness can protect from poverty, it is highly probable that the other MAVIS factors can grant a degree of protection against other adverse life events as well. For example, while having sex before marriage is a major risk factor for subsequent divorce across all social groups, the risk is significantly reduced in the case of people with a university education.(27)

But what happens to the vulnerable, those who do not possess many MAVIS factors? The poor, the physically unattractive, the depressed, the less intelligent and the men and women who do not rank high in the sexual attraction stakes do not have the same kind of protection against the adverse effects of sex outside of its intended purpose. Understandably, the pleasure principle can seduce these individuals, and they may easily think, “The film stars, rock stars, people in high places, etc. are doing it so it must be good.” But they do not have the same resources.

Population studies are a scientific tool used to see how specific groups fare when they are exposed to a specific behaviour. Population studies on the consequences of sex separated from a lifelong marriage between one man and one woman clearly support the moral teaching of Christianity. For example, these studies show that single motherhood is one of the leading obstacles to developing the full potential of women in the developed world.(28) They point to the escalating rates of sexually transmitted disease (STD).(29) Other such studies record appalling abortion statistics.(30) They also show that dramatic increases in mental health problems are associated with early multiple sexual exposures.(31) Figures for all these results are markedly higher among the less advantaged members of society.

Human beings suffer when they are not loved, and the most vulnerable suffer the most. Human beings gain immense pleasure from love, so nobody should be put in a position where their ability to obtain this gift is being adversely influenced by the actions of others. Even if an individual opts to sell himself or herself short, others who are more fortunate should try to prevent them from heading into this disaster. In a truly just society, it should be the duty of those around them who know a better deal to tell them about it, and this is done in the first place by being a good role model.

At least 1 in 3 first marriages, so about 33%, are formally divorcing.(32) One often-neglected question raised by this statistic is: what is happening in the other two-thirds who remain married? It is highly unlikely that there is a clear dividing line between couples who conclude "our marriage so bad it is time to divorce" and couples who consider that "our marriage is so good we shall stay together until death". Scientific investigations support this, along with common sense. Studies indicate that thoughts about divorce are common in married couples.

PG Parental guidance recommended

More than half of married individuals (ages 25–50) say they have had thoughts about divorce, either in the past or currently, based upon the fact that they consider life may be better with another partner. Divorce is of course contemplated when a relationship is failing, and a common feature of this mentality is perceiving that sexual gratification can be better elsewhere. (33)

However, when the cohort of people who have waited until marriage to have sex is looked at, a marked difference occurs. The divorce rate among this set of marriages is only 6% – about 1 in 16.(34) The study has not yet been performed on how many of these people think about divorce. But if only 6% are divorcing, is it likely that 50% of them are thinking about it?

To be scientifically correct, it is not possible to prove that avoiding sex before marriage actually causes marital stability. Correlation does not prove causation. It is possible that other factors are causing the stability, not least of which may be a sincere belief on the part of both partners that marriage is for life, and that includes tolerating behaviours which many would consider absolute indications for divorce and re-marriage, such as violence, addiction, and adultery.

However, even the Catholic Church, which is the most vocal opponent of divorce and remarriage, suggests separation often needs to be undertaken as a solution to these events. This usually requires a legal divorce to ensure that the innocent party and any children obtain just means of sustenance. Therefore, it is difficult to postulate that there is not at least some protective effect from virginity at the point of marriage.

PG Parental guidance recommended

As discussed in the previous chapter, some say it is good to have a lot of sexual partners before marriage, so you get used to trying people out and can find what you like. But this idea is not supported by the evidence, which is that if you get used to shopping around before marriage, you are developing a bad habit of "loving and leaving" that will make you more likely to divorce once married. And if it does not make you leave, it does make you more likely to wonder whether the "grass is greener on the other side", and therefore have less inner contentment.

This conclusion, that on the balance of probabilities keeping sex for marriage improves marital stability, has been drawn by numerous scientific investigations by social scientists using a wide variety of analytical methods and published in peer-reviewed journals – that is, scientific publications that are scrutinised for fairness and accuracy by other experts – over the past 30 years. To cite some:

- Kahn et al., 1991.(35) Data from the National Survey of Family Growth indicate that "women who are sexually active prior to marriage faced considerably higher risk of marital disruption than women who were virgin brides." These scholars explain that even when taking into account various differentials between virginal and non-virginal groups – such as socio economics, family background, attitudes and value differences – "non-virgins still face a much higher risk of divorce than virgins."

- Laumann et al., 1994.(36) This massive and highly respected National Health and Social Life

PG Parental guidance recommended

Survey, conducted at the University of Chicago, was the first serious, fully reputable study of sexual behaviour in America. It found a marked connection between premarital sex and elevated risk of divorce. The authors explain: “For both genders, we find that virgins have dramatically more stable first marriages...” Additionally, they conclude: “Those who marry as non-virgins are also more likely – all other things being equal – to be unfaithful over the remainder of their life compared with those spouses who do marry as virgins.”

- Teachman, 2003.(37) Sociologist Jay Teachman examined how premarital sex impacts risk of divorce among women. He found that “it remains the case, however, that women with more than one intimate relationship prior to marriage have an elevated risk of marital disruption.”

- Paik, 2011.(38) This study looked specifically at first sexual experience in adolescence and was conducted by Professor Anthony Paik at the University of Iowa. He made a particularly sad comment regarding consent. He explained, “Adolescent sexual debut that is not completely wanted is both directly and indirectly linked to marital dissolution.” What is more, he found that these experiences of not completely wanting to have sex are the experiences of the overwhelming majority of adolescent sexual encounters for girls. Seldom, in his study, was sexual consent completely free from at least a perceived pressure,

> due to the expectation that sex is an essential part of any boyfriend–girlfriend relationship. He also found that the overwhelming majority of non-virginal adolescent girls – nearly all – end up having had sex with multiple partners before marriage, thus increasing their risk for later divorce.

Young adults have a right to know about this sort of empirical information because of its very real potential impact on their later life.

Many people have had numerous sexual partners and yet have a lifelong marriage. Human resilience is remarkable in many situations where the odds are stacked against a good outcome. There are well-defined subsets of people who can withstand almost any adverse event and appear to come out on top! However, the risk of long-term unhappiness for the majority of the population is immense, and this information needs to be available to everybody so that their choice is truly free, and not muddled up with the idea that "sex is just sex". The evidence clearly proves that it is not!

Chapter 6

Scary words

Many words are used in the modern world to undermine traditional ideas about sex. They are words which on first hearing can sound like very convincing arguments for thinking that maybe the sexual revolution is a good thing. This is not true.

These words include:

- Choice
- Freedom
- Equality
- Discrimination
- Inclusiveness
- Diversity
- Consent

PG | Parental guidance recommended

Unguided choice as a tool to determine what is best for a person is simply crazy. All choices are not equivalent in outcome – the key is to discover the best. Few people would agree that cheating, concurrency (two or more sexual relationships at one time), excessive age differences, sugar-daddy sex, or many random partners are good for anybody, even though adult choice is involved. Accordingly, in reality everybody sets limits to choice that go beyond mere consent and safety. The key then is to set the limits according to what is truly best.

The correct choice should be based upon freedom. There is a freedom that all human beings enjoy, which is being free to do what we like. The problem is that that type of freedom is like a man who jumps off a cliff to enjoy the thrill of the fall. The jumper can enjoy the exhilaration of the decent, but he cannot escape the inevitable consequence of hitting the rocks below. The higher form of freedom, the type Jesus spoke about when he said that he had come to set us free, is being free to do what is best, and free from all manner of potential pitfalls.

Let's look at discrimination. From reason alone, most would accept that while a sign outside a public toilet saying "no black people allowed" is racist discrimination, a sign saying "men only" is not gender discrimination. Similarly, it is not offending against inclusiveness to restrict driving to those with good eyesight, even though this excludes blind people; or offending against the equality of children, for example, when a mother buys a new coat for her son but does not buy one for her daughter who has no need of one. Discrimination, Inclusiveness, and Equality are therefore rationally understood as assessments of proportionate purpose, not as mathematical sameness. All of these words are properly understood as a sensible balance between rights and responsibilities, not as a universal ticket to do anything based on a false concept of justice. This is how they should be used when speaking about sex.

Diversity is the understanding that each individual is unique, and it recognises the value of our individual differences. There are also necessary limits to diversity. Differences can be along the dimensions of race, ethnicity, gender, sexual orientation, socio-economic status, age, physical abilities, religious beliefs, political beliefs, or sexual behaviour. But tolerance or positive encouragement, in the name of diversity, for things that involve choice, cannot be unqualified. For example, respecting diverse religious beliefs is good, but if a religion's beliefs involve assaulting homosexual persons just for being homosexual, then this should not be either tolerated or (worse still) encouraged. It is the same with sexual behaviour. The limits of diversity are based on justice, as is apparent from reason.

Consent in the literal form is something every good-willed person cherishes. Nobody should be forced to do sexual acts that they do not want to do. But to jump from this statement to one that says the couple consented, so all is ok is absurd. Many factors are known to hide what one may call true consent versus visible consent. Fear, embarrassment, loneliness, depression, poverty and a host of other adverse life events impair the ability to make a true consent. Only consent in the context of an environment and psychological state that allows the person to seek the truth about what is best has any value.

Any thinking person recognises that every society in the world has had to set moral limits upon sexual behaviour for the wellbeing of individuals and society as a whole. It does not take much thought to realise that most people see that some lines need to be drawn. For example:

- while it may be legal to have 300 sexual partners, it is not good for public health in terms of sexually transmitted diseases
- while it may be legal to have two partners at once, most people agree that cheating is not good
- while it may be legal, there is something wrong when an 18-year-old girl books into a double-bed hotel room with her 75-year-old sugar-daddy

The debate then comes down to where the line should be drawn – this is true diversity. Jesus Christ drew the line at sex outside of marriage, and very good reasons can be shown why this should be so. Faith and reason go hand in hand on this.

Therefore, don't be scared of these words. They are words that every Christian cherishes – but used in the correct way.

PG Parental guidance recommended

Chapter 7

Do not be afraid

Jesus said, "Do not be afraid." (39) Many men and women who engage in sex outside of marriage suffer recurring fears. Jesus wants to take them all away.

For men:

Have I made her pregnant? Is it another month hoping her period will come? Why can't I just tell her I will not commit? Why am I infatuated with her? Does she cheat? Does she have a sexually transmitted infection? Do I need to go to the STD clinic for my annual check-up? Should we exchange HIV status checks before having sex? Will she try to trap me by getting pregnant? Will I marry the girl I do not really love because I feel bonded to her by sex? Am I being seduced? Why am I pretending to love her just to get sex? Why do I keep this area of my life

PG Parental guidance recommended

covered up? Why do I think I may ask her to have an abortion if she gets pregnant?

For women:

Am I pregnant? Will he stay with me if I am pregnant? Is abortion something I may have to contemplate? Has he got a sexually transmitted disease? Has he given me AIDS? Is he out with his friends tonight or is he cheating? Does he talk to his friends about my performance in bed? Why do I feel not completely at ease with my choice to have sex? Why do I feel the need to go along with it because everybody is doing it? Am I really consenting with my whole heart? Does he rank me against his previous girlfriends? Am I good enough at sex? Will he leave me if I do not have sex with him? I am getting older, I am late 20s/early 30s – will he look for a younger girl to marry? Will he commit to me or is this just a sex thing for him? Why am I giving sex just to get love? Is he just using me, and is marriage never part of his mind-set? Is he a man who loves sex with me but would only commit to a girl with higher social class or status? Will I ever get a boyfriend/husband if I say no to sex? Now that I'm getting older, will I have to lower my aspirations for the type of man I wish to marry so as not to be left single and alone? Will the only men left for single 30-something girls be divorcee men looking for a second-time-around opportunity? Why is my self-esteem so low? Why does my boyfriend, if he cares for me, ask me to do sexual things I really do not want to do?

PG | Parental guidance recommended

Chapter 8

The truth shall set you free

Jesus said, "The truth will make you free." (40) He came to set us free from the consequences of not following the will of God. We call being set free, "Redemption". Jesus sets us free from all kinds of pain, the most important of which is the pain of not going to heaven. Moreover, he sets us free from the pain caused by going against the will of God while we live here on earth. God's will is the will of a loving daddy for his children, he only knows what is best!

All manner of pains effecting the whole persona of an individual can be redeemed.

Psychological Pain

How often does one hear of single girls (in particular) suffering the effects of damaged sexual pairing after being caught up in a relationship where their partner did not really love them as they believed he did? They feel used, devalued, bitter, hardened, depressed, or distrustful of men. They have "spoken" the language of love only to find their love is not valued as it should be. Just read the letter pages in women's magazines, look at the shattered lives

of so many celebrities, or ask any general practitioner why so many people end up on anti-depressants.

How often do you see babies left to the care of (albeit often heroic) deserted, lonely, struggling single mothers? How often do you hear of single mums struggling to make ends meet? Each of these young girls was lied to big time – the man who "loved" her is nowhere to be seen.

There is more. How often do we see boys or girls who are clearly hitched to the wrong girl or guy but just cannot seem to get away because sex is bonding them together? "But I love him/her" is all they can say, even though the relationship is, obviously for all to see, going nowhere.

How often do you hear the regrets of young people who have embarked on sexual intercourse, got "hooked" by sex because of its intense ability to bond human beings, and only wish that they had said no? So many people carry in their heart the belief that sex should have been so different – they know that the girls or boys they have slept with do not deserve such a precious gift.

Physical Pain

How often do you hear of people with STDs? Having sex with someone means sleeping with their previous partners' infections!

Sadly, many young women who find themselves pregnant (often without any support from the father of the child) consider abortion to be the best solution. Abortion is all too often a consequence of male selfishness; the man just walks away. The woman unjustly carries the stigma and the responsibility.

PG Parental guidance recommended

From a physical perspective, termination of pregnancy is one of the safest surgical or medical procedures performed. It would be a lie to overstate the risk. However, it is not without risks, including the physical pain of the method utilised to terminate the pregnancy. Jesus does not want women to be exposed to threats to their health that can readily be avoided. Women are too valuable. Why should the culture of “If you get pregnant you can have an abortion” be thought acceptable? This is not good enough!

A number of specific complications of termination of pregnancy are quoted in medical studies, including the risk of reduced fertility, future miscarriage, and pelvic infection. The uterus is soft during pregnancy and it can be perforated either during dilation of the cervix or during suction, which are the methods most frequently used to terminate the life of the unborn child. These techniques also result in the possibility of damaging other structures in the pelvis, including the bowel and the bladder. The cervix may even tear during dilatation.

Everybody agrees that abortion is potentially a very difficult and painful decision for women to make. Even people who are in favour of abortion accept that some women are left psychologically traumatised by it. The only response they can offer is to ask whether there would be more psychological trauma if the abortion was not done. This is an impossible question to answer definitively using traditional scientific methods, because lifetime happiness and wellbeing are subject to so many confounding factors that no study can show this conclusively one way or the other. Is the woman who is depressed after an abortion depressed because of the abortion as such or due to a host of other adverse life

PG Parental guidance recommended

events in her life such as isolation, loneliness, poverty, or ridicule?

Nevertheless, is it likely that such a major life event in someone's life as killing an unborn child would not leave some profound pain (albeit hidden in the depths of the person's psyche)? We all experience varying degrees of anger, bitterness, confusion, guilt, depression, and other adverse emotions over things that we believe we could possibly have done differently if we had our time again. Why should abortion be any different? Women should not have to suffer this – there must be a better way.

Post-abortion trauma for men who realise that they did not try to support their pregnant girlfriend is an experience that is poorly studied. It is nevertheless well documented as a trauma for fathers of aborted babies.(41)

The pain of early exposure to sexual intercourse can even go into the genes! We now know that lifetime experiences can re-model genetic expression in a positive or negative way. The study of how life events change the ways our genes are turned on or off is called epigenetics. There are strong biological reasons to avoid sex before marriage because of the serious risk of adverse effects on genomic expression of not doing so. These are fully recognised by prestigious peer-reviewed journals that are not aligned to the moral teaching of the Church.(42) For example, it is known through epigenetics that it is possible for early exposure to sexual intercourse to turn on or off genes within a person's genome in a way that is contrary to the usual expression of those genes. The changes caused to the individual's genes by having multiple sexual partners adversely affect his or her lifelong performance in terms

PG | Parental guidance recommended

of both mental and physical attributes.(43) It is quite amazing that the Bible spoke about the sins of the father having consequences for the children, grandchildren, great grandchildren, etc., and epigenetics now seems to explain just how this happens!

Sex before marriage almost invariably involves the use of contraceptives. Modern contraceptives when used as instructed are highly effective at preventing pregnancy, but of course they are not 100% effective. Anybody having sex must recognise that pregnancy may occur. The Family Planning Association, who are very strong advocates for contraception, publish product failure rates.(44) The user failure rates are obviously much higher, as sex is a powerful distractor from thinking rationally, and poorly fitting condoms and caps plus missed pills are obvious results of this.

The pill	1% product failure rate
Condoms	2% product failure rate
Cap	4% product failurc rate

An important question to ask is: how safe are things like pills and coils? Again, to be honest, as medical treatments go, they are on the safe end of the spectrum, or they would not be so widely used. Nevertheless, they are not completely safe, so a legitimate question is, if one really cares for a person, why put that person at any risk whatsoever? For example, the contraceptive pill has a host of minor side effects such as weight gain, skin changes, and mood swings, to name just a few. In addition, there is a long list of rare but life-threatening complications including pulmonary embolisms, liver tumours, and breast cancer. The coil comes with the increased risk of pelvic infection and subsequent infertility. There is also an increased risk of any conception that occurs being ectopic (outside of the uterus), which constitutes a serious threat to the life of the mother if not dealt with swiftly.

Spiritual Pain

Last but not least is the spiritual damage of sex outside of marriage. It is clearly known from psychological experiments that most human communication occurs not by words but by body language. It is estimated that 55% of all communication occurs through body language, 38% by tone of voice and only 7% by the spoken word. (45)

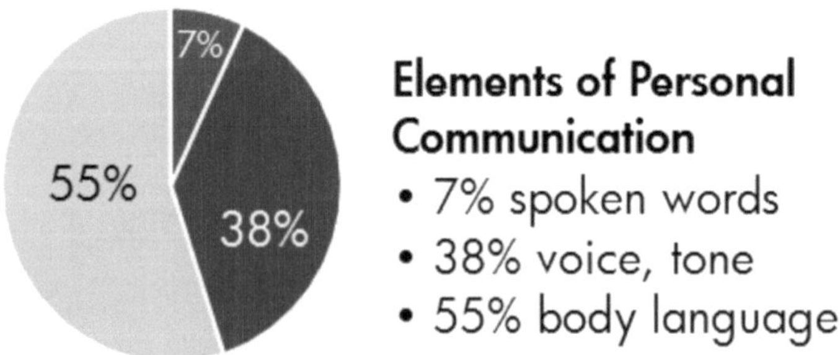

Sex is a very powerful body language. It communicates a strong sense of bonding and dependency. If "spoken" in

PG Parental guidance recommended

the wrong context, it can even distract some to the point of turning away from God. There is a real risk of developing a dependency on (a faith in) sex, and not God, as the source of our greatest love. How often have you heard things like, "I don't go to Mass anymore – the teaching of the Church about sex stuff is so outdated that I just don't believe the Catholic religion anymore!"

When Jesus spoke about losing the gift of heaven because of sex outside of marriage, it was because it is possible to desire sex more than God as the source of eternal happiness. It was also because it can be so harmful to one's partner, and the condition of going to heaven is to "love your neighbour as yourself."

Hell is the place where people who choose to place their faith in another source of greatest good, end up. It's not about God sending people to hell against their will, it's about God respecting the free will that we all have, because any loving relationship has to be able to choose. God loves us that much.

Trying to understand the pain of hell beyond the imagery of fire and brimstone is difficult. How can one imagine separating oneself from perfect love forever? One analogy used in an attempt to explain how bad this choice would be is that hell is the unending exposure to what each person placed their faith in as the source of eternal happiness, instead of what God revealed as the way to happiness.

Thus, in hell, people who put money first have loads of it in front of them, people who put position first have praise and adulation before them eternally, people who put power first have the opportunity to rule over others before them, and people who have been irretrievably distracted from faith in God by the allure of sexual gratification have this belief in sex before them 24/7. The problem is of course that none of these things really give eternal happiness, and ultimately, they are a torture, because the utter uselessness of these false gods is clear.

It is a very logical step to say that if the Church is wrong about something as important as sex, then she could be wrong about other matters of morality (right and wrong) and more importantly the faith in Jesus that she preaches. Not surprisingly therefore, opting for sex before marriage has a very strong correlation with giving up on the practice of Catholicism.

The joy of knowing Jesus as a friend walking beside us every day of our lives is a joy that cannot be replaced by sex. It is true that if the Church is wrong about this teaching concerning sex, she could just as easily be wrong about how to get to heaven. Jesus was so clear in his condemnation of sex outside of marriage that the Catholic Church cannot teach anything different. Heaven is just too good to miss. No amount of sex can equal it.

Free to... versus Free from...

It is very easy to get too focused on being free from. Looking at the negatives, being "free from", is a powerful tool to assist seeing the truth of the no-sex-before-marriage deal. But the positives, being free to, are even more valuable.

Being free to enjoy all manner of benefits when sex is kept for marriage is a subject that a whole book could be written about. In summary, dating and looking for Mr.

Right or Miss Right is a great thing to do. Avoiding sex while dating offers real freedom. The value of **being free to establish friendships** where time is spent talking and really getting to know the person and **being free to walk away with no regrets** when it is time to look for another boyfriend or girlfriend cannot be overstated.

We know that nobody is really a "loser" in God's eyes, and that God loves us all unconditionally – but let's be honest: many good people end up in relationships that are very unhealthy and even dysfunctional, and sex certainly can serve to keep couples together who really would be better off apart. Dating is about learning what kind of person would make a good marriage partner for you and parent for your children.

Dates where your mind is constantly preoccupied with worries about what is going to happen at the end of the night are sources of anxiety rather than what they are meant to be, namely a joyful adventure to find a spouse.

How far will he/she want to go? Will he/she help me to behave in the way I know is best? Will we go all the way tonight, next week, or next month? Chastity means keeping sex for marriage and using sex in marriage in a way that truly respects your husband or wife. Chastity does not stop when a gold ring is placed on the ring finger – it just changes in its demands. Chastity for the unmarried means one is free to date without the awkwardness of physical demands. When a couple choose chastity, they have the freedom to relax and be themselves around one another without worrying about what the other is expecting of them, physically.

The truth really can set you free!

PG Parental guidance recommended

PG Parental guidance recommended

Chapter 9

I keep on falling

Maybe you are already caught up in the whole sex thing in one way or another? Maybe you are sleeping around? Maybe you are a boy who is carrying the guilt of an abortion by facilitating one or walking away from your pregnant girlfriend? Maybe you are a single parent thinking, “Well, who would marry me now and set up a happy family?” Maybe you try to avoid getting too intimate with your boyfriend or girlfriend, but you repeatedly end up having sex? Maybe you are just about avoiding having sexual intercourse, but the physical intimacy is well on the way to intercourse, engaging in things like mutual masturbation, oral sex, sexting, sharing pornography and/or petting of erogenous (sexually stimulating) zones of the body?

You are right that no man (or woman) can sort this mess out completely, but Jesus is God and he sorts mess out big time! He brings “good out of evil”. The only condition is to try to love God. He is a saviour from mess! A transformer in modern speak. He just needs you to sincerely ask him to deliver you from these problems.

A famous painter once visited an expensive and exclusive restaurant. The waitress approached him with his soup, but being very nervous she spilt it all over the brilliant

PG Parental guidance recommended

white table cloth – it was a mess. The waitress could not apologise enough to this esteemed customer, and she expected to be condemned as stupid, incompetent, and banished to a lifetime of unemployment. But the artist heard her apology, smiled, and, using a spoon, converted the mess into a masterpiece that all could see. This is the type of transformation God can do.

In fact, God is doing it every day for those who try to love God. We are all in a mess in one way or another from the Pope down, so get your mess sorted out by Jesus today!

Saying no to sex before marriage, for example, even if you have slept with a thousand women or men before getting married, making a sincere commitment to change and getting God's seal of approval in the Sacrament of Confession, is like re-wrapping the gift of virginity for a future spouse. And if you fall again and again, Jesus just wants to pick you up.

Pope Francis summarised how God sees the person who is trying to do what is right versus the person who thinks they have cracked it and are good already. Nobody is good already. He said: "Let us remember that a small step, in the midst of great human limitations, can be more pleasing to God than a life which appears outwardly in order."(46)

The desire to find the special person, the soulmate to spend the whole of life with, is one of the greatest passions that human beings experience. It is a good thing, placed deep within us to ensure our happiness and the growth of the human race, so that God can generously share heaven with more and more people.

PG Parental guidance recommended

Particularly for girls, the pressure to conform with the expectation to sleep with a boyfriend or face the fear of being alone for life is something that can impair their ability to make a truly free choice. Men are in a more powerful position because 40-year-old men can find 30-year-old women to marry. But the biological clock works against women, and even if the biological clock did not exist, most men would still marry women younger than themselves.

To sin seriously, a person must be free. Duress and emotional instability can interfere with decision-making. Many young and not-so-young women secretly feel coerced into sleeping with men out of the fear of not getting a boyfriend and thus not being able to get married and have a family. God is a merciful Father, not a cruel taskmaster. He can heal the fear – just ask.

Unfortunately, it is impossible to devise a scientific study to prove the redemptive effects of trying to be chaste! The outcome study of those who make a choice to stop sex before marriage and then get married has not and cannot be done. Trying to recruit individuals in this cohort would be practically impossible. But from our faith we know that for those who really try to keep sex for marriage, even if they fall 1,000 times, the outcome will be good because Jesus promised that he would make all things new for those that love him.

PG Parental guidance recommended

Chapter 10

What is love?

A lot has been spoken about love. Next time or the first time your boyfriend or girlfriend says, “I love you”, try this little quiz. Ask him or her, what does he or she mean?

True love means? (circle the correct answer)

ANSWER 1	AGAPE	YES/NO
ANSWER 2	EROS	YES/NO
ANSWER 3	EPITHUMIA	YES/NO

PG Parental guidance recommended

Jesus did not speak English! In English we have only one word for love. I can love pizza, my mum, my football club, or my girlfriend. Hopefully, the love for a girlfriend is different to the love for a pizza!

The three different words for love offered above have the following meanings:

Agape	Self-sacrifice
Eros	Mutual needs
Epithumia	Self-satisfaction

What Jesus meant by the word love is "*agape*", self-sacrificing love. This is the word used in the gospels that were first written in Greek. *Agape* is the highest form of love, sacrificial love, love that puts the other person's needs above one's own. It is real love. This is what Jesus revealed to us as the secret to happiness. Sadly, the word love and the act of love are all too frequently reduced to things other than *agape*.

"*Epithumia*", self-gratification, is just a caricature of love. It means using someone, leading them on, while really being concerned only about one's own wellbeing. It is also called lust. It is making someone believe they are cared for when they are not. Sadly, it often goes under the name of love. Many vulnerable people are deceived when they are told "I love you" when what is really meant is "I want you for *epithumia* and that's it!"

"*Eros*", or mutual need, is also a common substitute for real love, the love that we all crave for and that, as God himself revealed to us by his life, would make us happy. *Eros* is a good starting point, but it cannot be the end point. When one starts dating, many mutual needs are satisfied, such as conversation, companionship, shared interests, and a sense of excitement in discovering whether he/she is the one. However, it needs to move on from *eros* to *agape* if it is to flourish.

Have you ever heard that you are made in the "image and likeness of God"?(47) It is very easy to read this and imagine it means that God looks like us, or that he is a kindly old man with a beard. These words that are translated from the original language of the Bible as "image and likeness" have much deeper meaning. "Image" means that we resemble God in that we can freely decide to do good by loving as God loves. "Likeness" means that like God, who has control of all of creation, we have been given a degree of control of the world around us; this is called dominion. The secret of happiness is to practise *agape* in the world around us.

Christ showed by his life the secret to human fulfilment. He told us to "love one another as I have loved you." His life was the clearest demonstration of what God's love really means. This is how we obtain happiness. If any animal is going to thrive, it needs to act according to its nature. A lion needs to hunt antelopes. If a lion is denied the hunt, the lion lacks fulfilment. Just look at how unhappy lions are in a zoo. Similarly, human beings have the nature of being made in the image and likeness of God – we need to receive *agape* if we want to be truly happy. And if we need to receive it, it is a reasonable expectation that we should give it as well. It is a paradox, absurd but true, that Christ revealed to us that the more we serve others and the more we give to others, the richer and happier we become. It goes against the laws of economics. It sounds crazy, like saying if we give away £100 we become richer – but it's true!

PG | Parental guidance recommended

PG Parental guidance recommended

Chapter 11

Isn't this sex stuff just Catholic repression and Catholic guilt?

It is often said that Catholics are repressed or suffer unhealthy guilt when it comes to sex.

Repression as a psychological process can undoubtedly be a harmful thing. But Catholics are not into repression, they are into transformation.

The word “passion” in ordinary language has different meanings, from a hobby to the drive to do something or even your major life target. Historically, however, passions were understood as the strong emotional forces that suggest to us to perform a specific behaviour. Christ's passion, for example, was to suffer and die for us.

Catholics are not people who think all passions, including the passion of sexual desire, are bad or sinful. Similarly, Catholics don't think every passion must be expressed in the way any individual chooses. Passions need to be used for good. We should be passionate people in the best sense of the word! God made human beings passionate, so passions must be good things. Just look at the human

PG Parental guidance recommended

passions that everybody agrees are universal to the human race, and see what good uses and bad uses they can be put to. The passions of hatred, sadness, fear, desperation, anger and desire (sexual or non-sexual) have much good to offer, but sadly can all too easily become harmful! For example, it's good to be angry at injustice, but it's not good to be angry with people when they make trivial mistakes. It's good to be sad when we see the pain and suffering of a fellow human being, but it's highly damaging to fall into prolonged, excessive sadness when faced with adverse challenges in our own lives; that is how to develop a depressive illness. Likewise, the passion of sexual desire needs to be used for good purposes.

Concerning the so-called "Catholic guilt", it has been suggested that one of the reasons Catholics will not have sex before marriage is because of a destructive guilt complex embedded by the Church in its adherents after their minor sexual misdemeanours. The term "Catholic guilt" can be used to pressure young Catholics, who have been brought up to believe that keeping sex for marriage is a wise choice, into changing their minds and having sex before marriage.

Now, guilt can be viewed in terms of constructiveness versus destructiveness. Constructive guilt is focused on recognising one's moral lapses, seeking forgiveness for them, changing one's behaviour, and using the memory of the guilt to help avoid another episode in the future. This is a good thing. Conversely, destructive guilt keeps the person mired in self-loathing, unable to learn from his or her wrongdoings to move ahead in life. This is a bad thing. Catholics, like everybody, can fall prey to destructive guilt, but it is not part of Catholic Christianity.

PG | Parental guidance recommended

Chapter 12

What is so special about Marriage?

It may seem strange to ask the question, "What is so special about marriage?" But sadly, this question does need to be asked. Marriage is a unique type of friendship that is defined by very specific criteria which in many ways have been forgotten or distorted. As a result, there is a very understandable belief that living together, or even polyamorous care partnerships and marriage are very similar types of relationships that are of equal value.

While there are many reasons why couples decide to move in and delay or avoid marriage, one of the usual reasons is to facilitate sexual relations. Moving into the same address in itself is not an issue, provided adequate steps are made to avoid having sex. Many engaged couples, in many different cultures, over many centuries for example, have lived with their in-laws prior to marriage, most commonly for economic reasons. But usually it is wise to avoid the same address to avoid temptation.

Until recently, the word marriage had the same meaning for everyone. If you asked an English person in 1930,

PG | Parental guidance recommended

regardless of any religious belief, what marriage was, they would say marriage was a man and a woman living together for the whole of their lives, sexually exclusive, with unconditional commitment, and if possible being open to having and bringing up children.

The words of the marriage ceremony, the wedding vows, are the means of asking the couple about the essential components of the unique friendship called Christian marriage. As an aide-memoire, they are the AEIOUs.

Affinity	*A complementary and reciprocal relationship of one man and one woman - "Do you Sarah take this man John as your lawfully wedded husband?"*
Exclusive	*No cheating - "forsaking all others"*
Indissoluble	*No divorce and re-marriage - "until death do us part"*
Open to children	*Desire to have children - "live according to God's law"*
Unconditional	*Unqualified love – "for better or worse, for richer or poorer..."*
Sacramental	*God's power is invoked in the blessing of the couple; they are asked to join in with this request for grace by saying "Amen"*

PG Parental guidance recommended

Marriage is an ontological fact. Ontology means something that is just in the bones; it is part of our nature as human beings. It is like man desires to be loved and give love – it is in the depths of our being. Love is what makes the world go round! The promises made are reflections of deep inner desires in the heart of men and women to be happy. It is very different from any other type of friendship or human-to-human relationship.

INNER (ONTOLOGICAL) CALL TO MARRIAGE	***WHAT THE HEART IS SAYING***
Affinity	*"I want to be with you"*
Reciprocity	*"I know I can be good for you because our physical self, our psychological self and spiritual self are made for each other"*
Complementariness	*"I know you and I together will always make something bigger than both of us just added together"*
Exclusivity	*"I want only you"*
Indissolubility	*"I want to be with you always until I die"*
Procreativity	*"I would like to see another you in the world"*
Unconditionality	*"I want to give you my all"*

PG Parental guidance recommended

There has been a massive change in our culture concerning the understanding of the word marriage. The Christian understanding of marriage has been undermined in many ways in our society by things that are just casually spoken about as being a normal part of modern marriage. Christians live in the world, and the world has powerful means to corrupt belief and understanding.

For example, divorce and remarriage are so common it is not surprising that the concept of no divorce, i.e. Indissolubility, is poorly recognised.

Our newspapers and magazines speak openly about “Pre-Nuptial Agreements”, i.e. public statements of conditions placed upon a “marriage”, so we should not be surprised at the Unconditionality of love being debatable.

As for Exclusivity, the media spend huge amounts of time and effort reporting on celebrity marriages when one or other partner is committing adultery and espousing the value of open relationships. Sadly, “a little bit on the side” is even joked about as if it were something trivial. Also the promulgation of polyamorous partnerships (open marriages) as a solution to the demands of monogamy just hide the sadness of jealousy and feelings of being in a competition for affection which get worse year on year as aging occurs.

On a similar note, in terms of having children, not an eyebrow would be raised if a couple approached a registry office saying that they never want to have children, even if they are able and can afford to do so. Not many people nowadays would accept the idea that a fertile couple getting married must be open to the possibility of

PG Parental guidance recommended

procreating and rearing children, or that this openness to children is a defining element of marriage. In a society that upholds contraception as an absolute moral good, it would hardly occur to anyone that the intention to have a childless marriage for reasons of personal comfort could be contrary to the true understanding of marriage.

Making the union of a woman and a man public and protected by law is very important, because it is a very powerful mechanism to protect the rights of the parties involved. We all make sure that important things, for example, buying a house or adopting a child, are formally recognised. These things are not just left to private arrangements where nobody else is called upon to witness them on behalf of society at large. Lifelong intimate relationships are no less important.

Historically, the Church has opposed "common law marriages" "moving-in" "cohabitation" because of the serious threat they posed especially to the wellbeing of women and children. This is just the same today. They are agreements with varying degrees of rights and responsibilities that leave too much scope for misunderstanding and readjustment of the responsibilities that intimate relationships should have as inalienable features. Women and children deserve the best.

Many people nowadays say that it is having children together and/or taking out a mortgage together that really shows commitment, not obtaining a piece of paper, having a gold ring and/or throwing an expensive party. This is probably very true if marriage is just a piece of paper to the couple! There is probably more commitment in the bank document or the birth certificate! But real marriage is much more.

Many Catholics, including the Pope, recognise that some long-term living together relationships show many features of commitment that may be lacking in some relationships labelled as marriage. (48) The Pope himself has honestly questioned whether many Church marriages are truly marriages, as some couples have not entered into them with a proper understanding of permanence and commitment.(49)

But true marriage is about the best commitment. To put it simply, it is the difference between a Rolls-Royce and a 20-year-old Subaru. Both cars may take us on the trip of a lifetime, but all the evidence is that the trip is more comfortable, more secure, more reliable and safer in the Rolls-Royce. For a Catholic, this is primarily because marriage has God using his power, called grace, to assist the relationship. It is called a Sacrament.

A true understanding of marriage obviously sets the bar high; it means that getting married is a major step to take. It calls for a clear decision. And choosing to marry is the point when we get to decide. Marriage is an institution, which is public, "for life", and requires perhaps the highest-quality decision of our lives.

The problem with the alternatives to marriage is that, because the bar is set lower, it is too easy to drift in and out, avoiding real decisions. If the consequences of failure really were minor, then a "try it and see" attitude might make sense. But in fact, immense hurt comes from intimacy broken and rejected. Marriage alone provides a safe context for intimacy so that we can let our hearts lead

PG Parental guidance recommended

us without fear of being wounded in the process. Commitment is safety. Without that safe context, we are potentially setting ourselves (and our partners) up for a fall. Sadly, a series of falls can very easily lead to bitterness and depression.

Many people fear getting married. One of the big factors here is fear of failure, which has been fanned by the experience of family breakdown over the last two generations. In particular, those who have witnessed the breakdown of their parents' relationship will often carry a wound, which creates a deep nervousness about committing. Others will be influenced by family breakdowns they have seen in their circle of friends or their extended family. Because family breakdown is so commonplace, the fear will have joined with the reality to make people doubly anxious.

Our contemporary culture has done us all a great disservice by taking the problem of unstable relationships, which is real, and making it worse by undermining true marriage as the best answer to that instability, by facilitating all the things that go against its defining criteria. Legalising divorce and re-marriage, encouraging the use of contraception and child free marriages, accepting pre-nuptial agreements at least in some jurisdictions, and sometimes trivialising adultery and "open marriages" all help to compromise the true meaning of marriage.

A happy marriage is best prepared for by understanding what it really means to take marriage vows, and by avoiding sex before marriage. Studies do tend to point to all manner of "happiness markers" being better for couples who abstained from sex before their

PG Parental guidance recommended

marriage.(50) These happiness markers include very significant improvements in:

- Relationship stability
- Relationship satisfaction
- Quality of sexual intercourse
- Communication

Premarital cohabitation (moving in and living together) has increased significantly in recent times. The major argument supporting premarital cohabitation is that it enables the couple to get know each better and to see whether they get along well enough to embark on marriage and obviously to have sex! However, counter-intuitively, many studies, as noted above, have found that premarital cohabitation is associated with increased risk of divorce, lower quality of marriage and poorer marital communication.

To be fair, more recent studies although few in number seem to refute the negative correlation. This has led some to say living together is a good idea. The real reason for this seemingly opposite result is that all studies are done on people who have varying degrees of contamination by the prevailing culture around them. This means that even a couple who abstain from pre-marital intercourse are at risk of being influenced by the many factors around them that undermine their marital commitment, such as professionals who are often considered incorrectly to be wise in all things advocating divorce as a solution to marital disharmony. As society becomes more and more averse to real marriage everybody is at risk of being contaminated.

A big question for many is why is cohabitation and sex

PG Parental guidance recommended

before marriage so risky for many couples regarding future marital stability when it can sound absurd, especially to those who have managed to live together and come out of it unscathed?

The simple answer is that resilience is a feature that can correct even the most adverse events. Resilience is related to exposure to protective factors. These factors are things that protect their relationship, such as having two loving parents who are married, brought up in a secure home, have a good education and financial security. Conversely, in the moving-in/sex before marriage group who land up with failed relationships there is a disproportionate number of couples who lack many protective factors such being younger and less mature, have weaker family ties, poorer socio-economic standing and are not so well educated.

Also, every couple who choose to engage in sex before marriage are unique. They range from those who really want to get married to those who have zero long term commitment to each other with all variations in between the extremes. Therefore, any study is fraught with problems because it is impossible to know how many of each group is being studied.

Marriage is very special. It makes real Families with a capital F. In our society, we use the word "family" in an analogical sense when we talk about a "family" of trees, plants, flowers, etc. Similarly, we use the word "family" in human relations to describe a father, two children and a new live-in girlfriend, or a mother, one child and the fourth husband who is labelled as a stepdad, and countless other combinations; but this is by analogy to the real thing, not as equivalence in terms of human fulfilment. They share some features of the real Family but not all. The people in these relationships are often in this situation due to a host of complicated and difficult life scenarios – it is not for anybody to make adverse subjective judgements about their behaviour, past or present.

Family with a capital F is the result of a man and a woman freely choosing to marry. It would be best to call it the marriage family, but we shorten it to family. It establishes a web of relationships, closest with the couple themselves and their children, and spreading out to grandparents, cousins, etc.

The best deal has been testified to by the millions of people over the centuries who have led fulfilled lives because of marriage and Family with a capital F. No alternative has been shown to be better for the couple themselves, for society, and for children. The outcomes in terms of health, wealth, longevity, educational achievement and numerous other quality measures are there for all to see as the wise socialist commentator at the start of this book.

From reason alternatives to marriage for embarking upon an intimate sexual relationship are clearly not good enough. Many think these alternative options are as good as it gets due to a loss of confidence in the institution of marriage, but this is not true. Human beings are made for real love that is found in real marriage.

Just imagine the offer of the polyamorous man: "Hi, will you live with me and my other three partners whom I need to prioritise when necessary?" Similarly, imagine the offer from a prospective moving-in boyfriend: "Hi,

PG | Parental guidance recommended

will you live with me and if I think you are worth it, we can stay together? If not, I shall move on and try someone else." Along the same type of reasoning comes the offer of union from the person where divorce enters the mind-set: "Hi, will you marry me until death do us part; I mean, of course until the death of our relationship, if that should occur before my physical death!" Or the offer from a peripatetic father: "Hi, will you have a relationship with me, but I am not signed up to caring for any children that I generate." And, last but most certainly not least, the offer from a woman who is not open to children, or a man not prepared to shoulder his responsibilities: "Hi, let us get together, but if pregnancy occurs, then it is time for an abortion as I do not want your children."

Only marriage can offer the best deal possible.

PG Parental guidance recommended

Chapter 13

Where does a parent start?

For many parents, it can seem an almost impossible task to encourage a "no sex before marriage" option with their children because sex before marriage is so common, or because the parents themselves opted for this lifestyle when they were young. Feelings of being a hypocrite can easily overcome the desire to speak the truth.

Remember that being a good Catholic means recognising our weaknesses and hypocrisy and trying to change. Jesus pointed out the difference in attitude between a Publican

PG Parental guidance recommended

(a man who recognised his weakness and wanted to change) and a Pharisee (a man who thought he had "made it" in terms of his relationship with God.) You only have a problem if you think you do not need to say to God "I messed up, I am like the Publican, I need you God to save me!"

The best advice is to be honest. We all learn as the years go on, we all have had life experiences where, if we had our time again, we would have done things differently.

Simply say that you want what is best for your children because the longer you live, the more and more you love them. And whatever they do, you will always love them.

As for your children, give them the tools they need to negotiate a world saturated in sex. Maybe this little book may help them find the words to hold onto the truth of what is best for them.

PG Parental guidance recommended

Conclusion

Sadly, Catholic Christianity is often perceived as a series of no's. Catholics say no to sex before marriage, no to masturbation, pornography, divorce, and a long list of other sex-related topics. In reality, though, being a Catholic Christian means having a close, loving relationship with Jesus. The laws are only necessary because we can sometimes forget how to love, so they act as a safety net.

It is like this. Hopefully your mother did not need laws to tell her that child abuse was wrong – she just loved you, and as an inevitable consequence, no abuse ever occurred.

When we fall in love with Jesus, because that is what Catholic Christianity is about, his will becomes our will. The laws are no longer required. When Jesus was teaching about the reasons people cannot go to heaven, it was with great sadness on his face. This is because he desperately wants what is best for us. This book is an attempt to prove just how much he really cares by giving evidence to support his teaching concerning sex before marriage.

In any loving relationship, we are judged by the standard of how much we have loved. Sex separated from marriage has the potential to hurt others and ourselves in a myriad of ways. Therefore, it is so serious in God's eyes because love is the measure he expects from us.

Loving God, and loving our neighbour as ourselves, were not new ideas preached by Jesus. These commands were well known to the Jewish people hundreds of years before Jesus walked on earth. (51)(52)

What was new was that Jesus linked the two. He made it clear that our love for God and our understanding of how much God loves us will be measured by how much we love our neighbour.

It would be a grave misunderstanding to read this book and conclude that the definition of good Catholic girls / boys is that they do not have sex before marriage and bad Catholic girls / boys do have sex before marriage. Going to Mass, not having sex before marriage and being involved in parish life are all good things, but they are not a guaranteed ticket to heaven!

Jesus told his disciples that there will be people at the threshold of heaven, claiming to have done great things in his name, only to be told, “I never knew you” (53).

Since religious activity can be the product of behaviour modification to make us feel good, taken by itself it is not a reliable indicator of our spiritual state. Basing our spiritual health solely on religious activity is like basing our physical health solely on physical activity. While diminished physical activity can be indicative of a serious medical condition, often it is not. Some people are very sedentary but live to be 100. Similarly, there have been top athletes who have competed at the highest level while harbouring a virulent, undetected cancer. In the same way, religious activity alone, despite fervour, may mask a crumbling relationship with God.

Often discovering our true state of physical health requires that we undergo intrusive procedures — blood

PG Parental guidance recommended

tests, colonoscopies, pelvic examinations, and mammograms — involving needles, x-rays, scopes, and probes that can be uncomfortable, painful, and embarrassing. Understanding our spiritual health requires an equally intrusive and sometimes unpleasant procedure: probing beneath the surface of religiosity into our heart — the attitudes and motivations that shape what we are and what we do.

Given that Jesus regarded "fruits" as the touchstone of spiritual health, it is good to check out how fruitful we are. Fruits of the Spirit are a character marked by a spirit (life) of love, joy, peace, patience, kindness, goodness, faithfulness, gentleness, and self-control. To test those fruits, we might ask ourselves, for example:

- Is our attitude toward our enemies loving?
- Do we find it easy to experience joy when things aren't going our way?
- Do we really want peace in the world, a harmony that in part requires sacrificing our own material wellbeing in the pursuit of justice?
- Do we have patience with frustrating people?
- Do we have tender, gentle compassion for those who are sleeping with their boyfriend/girlfriend, or are we conceited and judgemental?
- Are we kind to unkind people?
- Are we faithful to the things we know are true?
- Do we try to say no to harmful thoughts and temptations?

Maybe after reading this little book you are still questioning. Perhaps you think, "If I created a population and a world for them to live in, I wouldn't expect them to

PG
Parental guidance recommended

love me in the way I instruct, especially if I didn't show myself to them and I gave them free will. And I wouldn't punish them for not loving me either, that would be evil. I mean, you don't go around punishing people for not loving you, you just appreciate the love you get, don't you? And for those who don't love you, if you really were nice, you would forgive them and say let bygones be bygones. Therefore, I don't need to do the will of an external law-maker rather than my own. Why would you need everyone to love you just because you're God?"

These thoughts lead many to say, "I shall just follow my conscience" rather than saying, "I shall follow my Jesus-informed conscience." Many people have had an image of God portrayed to them that is far from an all-loving daddy. Sadly, the attitude of supposedly religious people may have had a part to play. Therefore, there are a lot of reasons to compassionately understand the thought process of sex life being an irrelevancy to the God–man relationship.

However, the above analysis about God's creation, his need for love, and his remoteness is not the true picture.

God has truly revealed himself to human beings both in the depths of our reason (there is something bigger than us out there) and most clearly by God himself entering human history 2024 years ago in the person of Jesus Christ. And why does he desire our love? It is because God revealed his nature, that which gives him fulfilment. Lions can only hunt for food; they cannot farm, although both provide sustenance. God can only seek love; domination, dictatorship, capriciousness, sycophancy, and self-adulation all form some sort of relationship, but it is not love, hence he just cannot do it. And the love of a daddy demands the free will of the children (you and me) to say yes or no to a relationship. Love is never forced.

At times it can appear to be an overwhelming task to live as Jesus asked us to live. Mary, Our Lady, is our mother and she can untie knots that appear impossible to untie, as only a mother can! Just ask her! Here in England, we are privileged to have one of the oldest Marian shrines in the world at Walsingham. Many have heard of places linked to Mary, like Our Lady of Lourdes and maybe Our Lady of Fatima and Our Lady of Guadalupe. But our shrine is hundreds of years older. Ask Our Lady of Walsingham to pray for you.

England is historically known as Mary's Dowry. King Richard II named England Mary's Dowry almost 1,000 years ago. Remember, England was a 100% Catholic country, and that included everyone from the King down. "Dowry" means a present, a gift of valuable property. The wonderful love that burned within the hearts of our forefathers towards the Mother of God in England is the great present this country offered to her. In return, she has asked God for countless blessings for our country. By contributing to this dowry, this present of love for his mother, you can make sure that Jesus will be eager to answer your prayers, even when it appears an almost impossible request.

PG Parental guidance recommended

References

1. Furedi, Ann. (2014) Women trying hard to avoid unwanted pregnancy. London: British Pregnancy Advisory Services Publications 4th February 2014

2. Dennis, N. and Halsey, A. H. (1988) *English Ethical Socialism.* 1st Edition. Oxford: Clarendon Press

3. The CTS New Catholic Bible. (2008) 1st Edition. 1 Peter 3:15-16. London: Catholic Truth Society

4. The CTS New Catholic Bible. (2008) 1st Edition. Gospel of St. Mark 7:14-23. London: Catholic Truth Society

5. Hoffmann, R. (1987) Celsus. On the True Doctrine, a Discourse Against the Christians. 1st Edition. Oxford: Oxford University Press Incorporated

6. The CTS New Catholic Bible. (2008) 1st Edition. Gospel of St. John 1:1-14. London: Catholic Truth Society

7. The CTS New Catholic Bible. (2008) 1st Edition. Gospel of St. John 2:19. London: Catholic Truth Society

8. Polano, H. (2003) *The Talmud* (translated) 1st Edition. London: Book Tree Publisher

9. Keller, W. (1955) *The Bible as History.* 1st Edition. London: Hodder and Stoughton

PG Parental guidance recommended

10. The CTS New Catholic Bible. (2008) 1st Edition. Gospel of St. Luke 3:1. London: Catholic Truth Society

11. Habermas, G. (1996) *The Historical Jesus: Ancient Evidence for the Life of Christ*. 1st Edition. Joplin: College Press Publishing Company

12. Vatican Council II *Dei Verbum*. (1996) 3rd Edition Dublin: Dominican Publications

13. Bruce, F. (1974) *Jesus and Christian Origins Outside the New Testament*. 1st Edition. Grand Rapids Michigan: William B. Eerdmans Publishing Company

14. Stevenson, R. (1991) (first published 1886). *The Strange Case of Dr. Jekyll and Mr. Hyde*. Milwaukee USA: Dover Publications

15. See The CTS New Catholic Bible. (2008) 1st Edition. Romans 7:19-20. London: Catholic Truth Society

16. The CTS New Catholic Bible. (2008) 1st Edition. 1 John 4:8. London: Catholic Truth Society

17. Pope Francis. (2016) *The Name of God is Mercy*. 1st Edition. New York: Penguin Random House

18. British sex survey 2014 accessed on line at: https://www.theguardian.com/lifeandstyle/2014/sep/28/british-sex-survey-2014-nation-lost-sexual-swagger (accessed January 2 2018)

19. Office for National Statistics Divorce in England and Wales 2016. Accessed on line at:

PG Parental guidance recommended

https://www.gov.uk/.../statistics/divorces-in-england-and-wales-2016 (accessed January 2 2018)

20. Abortion Rates in the UK. *The Guardian* (newspaper) 9th August 2006

21. Office for National Statistics. Families and Households 2014. UK Government Publications

22. British sex survey 2014 accessed on line at: https://www.theguardian.com/lifeandstyle/2014/sep/28/british-sex-survey-2014-nation-lost-sexual-swagger (accessed January 2 2018)

23. Greer, G. (1970) *The Female Eunuch*. 1st Edition. USA: McGraw-Hill

24. Greer, G. (1984) *Sex and Destiny*. 1st Edition. New York: Harper and Row

25. Ben ZE'ev, A (2001) *The Subtlety of Emotions* 1st Edition. Massachusetts: MIT Press

26. Hakim, C. (2012) *Honey Money - The Power of Erotic Capital*. 1st Edition. London: Penguin Press

27. Casey, E. et al. National Health Statistics - First Marriages in the USA. National Health Statistics Report Number 49, 22 March 2012

28. Joseph Rowntree Foundation. (2007) *Parenting and poverty*. 1st Edition. UK: York Publishing Services Ltd

29. Public Health England. (2017) *Sexually transmitted infections (STIs): surveillance, data, screening, and management.* 2nd Edition. London: PHE Publications

30. Department of Health. (2017) Abortion statistics, England and Wales. Accessed on line at: https://www.gov.uk/government/collections/abortion-statistics-for-england-and-wales (accessed November 2, 2017)

31. Hallfors, D.D. et al. (2005) Which comes first in adolescence—sex and drugs or depression? *American Journal of Preventative Medicine*, 29 (2005): 163-170

32. Office for National Statistics Divorce in England and Wales 2016. Accessed on line at: https://www.gov.uk/.../statistics/divorces-in-england-and-wales-2016 (accessed January 2, 2018)

33. Hawkins, A. et al. How many married people have thought about divorce? Institute for Family Studies, November 2, 2015

34. Wolfinger, N. Counterintuitive trends in link between premarital sex and marital stability. Institute for Family Studies, June 6 2016

35. Kahn, J.R. et al. "Premarital Sex and the Risk of Divorce," *Journal of Marriage and Family*, 53 (1991): 845-855

36. Laumann, E et al. (1994) *The Social Organization of Sexuality: Sexual Practices in the United States*. 1st Edition. Chicago: University of Chicago Press

37. Teachman, J. "Premarital Sex, Premarital Cohabitation, and the Risk of Subsequent Marital Dissolution Among Women." *Journal of Marriage and Family* 65 (2003): 444-455

38. Paik, A. "Adolescent Sexuality and Risk of Marital Dissolution," *Journal of Marriage and Family* 73 (2011)

39. The CTS New Catholic Bible. (2008) 1st Edition. Gospel of St. Matthew 28:10. London: Catholic Truth Society

40. The CTS New Catholic Bible. (2008) 1st Edition. Gospel of St. John 8:32. London: Catholic Truth Society

41. Coyle, C.T. (1999) *Men and Abortion. A path to Healing*. 1st Edition. New York: Lifecycle Books

42. Anderson, J. (2016) *The Teenage Brain Under Construction*. 2nd Edition. American College of Paediatricians. Accessed on line at: https://www.acpeds.org/the-college-speaks/position-statements/parenting-issues/the-teenage-brain-under-construction (accessed October 28 2017)

43. Berger S. L. et al. "An operational definition of epigenetics". *Genes and Development*, 23 (2009): 781-783

44. "Your Guide to Contraception". Family Planning Association Publications. October 2008

45. Mehrabian, A. (1981) *Silent Messages: Implicit Communication of Emotions and Attitudes*. 2nd Edition. Belmont: Wadsworth Publishers

PG Parental guidance recommended

46. Pope Francis. (2016) Apostolic Exhortation *Amoris Laetitia*. London: Catholic Truth Society

47. See the CTS New Catholic Bible. (2008) 1st Edition. Genesis 1:26. London: Catholic Truth Society

48. Pope Francis. (2016) *Amoris Laetitia*. London: Catholic Truth Society

49. Pope Francis. Speech at the Opening of the Pastoral Congress of the Diocese of Rome, 16 June 2016. https://www.catholicnewsagency.com/news/34056/updated-most-marriages-today-are-invalid-pope-francis-suggests (accessed December 26 2017)

50. Busby, D. et al. "Compatibility or restraint? The effects of sexual timing on marriage relationships", *Journal of Family Psychology*, 24 (2010): 766

51. The CTS New Catholic Bible. (2008) 1st Edition. Deuteronomy 6:5. London: Catholic Truth Society

52. The CTS New Catholic Bible. (2008) 1st Edition. Leviticus 19:18. London: Catholic Truth Society

53. The CTS New Catholic Bible. (2008) 1st Edition. Gospel of St. Matthew 7:23. London: Catholic Truth Society